Oh No!
Not Another Problem

A Practical Approach To Solve Day-to-Day Problems

- The Barking Dog
- Retirement – A New Start
- 36, Single And Looking
- I Want – You Provide
- Stay In The Job Or Quit
- Suddenly A Widow

12/5/00

For Mary
Enjoy
at the request
of Barbara Cem
Jeanette Griver

JEANETTE A. GRIVER
MICHELE W. VODREY

Michele W. Vodrey

Compsych Systems, Inc.
A Human Factors Company
Marina del Rey, California

Library of Congress Catalog Card Number 00 092436

Griver, Jeanette A. and Vodrey, Michele W.
- Oh No! Not Another Problem — A Practical
  Approach To Solve Day-to-Day Problems

ISBN 0-929948-02-5 (hard copy)
ISBN 0-929948-03-3 (pbk.)

Printed in the United States by Eastwood Printing, Denver, Colorado.

Illustrations by Ann Cleaves

In Memory
Of
Dave and George

Acknowledgments

To Phyllis Milway for her discerning editing and sustained energy.

To Mary Kay Boyd, John Espey, George Katz, J.D., Ph.D, James T. Milway and Carolyn See, Ph.D, who challenged the clarity of our concepts.

To Donna Bane, Barbara Carr, Tessy Maehler, Mike Michelson and Anthony Raciti for their review and suggestions.

To Margot B. Robinson, Ph.D, and Raymond Frankel, colleagues and friends whose original research on the Griver-Robinson-Frankel theory of "Motivated Learning Through Structured Feedback" provided the basis of many ideas in the book.

A special thank you to the thousands of people who have participated in programs we have presented on problem analysis and communication skills.

Contents

Introduction

How many times have you said, "Oh no, not another problem"? The thought of having to deal with one more problem or make one more decision can overwhelm you. Sometimes you do nothing; other times you rely on your past experiences and make quick decisions. It would be ideal if you could turn to a textbook, similar to one used for chemistry, in which you could find measurable answers and formulas to help solve a problem.

Although there isn't an exact formula that will guarantee a solution to your problems, *Oh No! Not Another Problem* provides you with a basic and objective process, *operational analysis,* that you can apply to solve a range of day-to-day or uncommon problems. *Operational analysis* is the organized collection of facts which reveals the measurable dimensions (**who, what, when, where, how, why and costs**) of problems that are originally described in vague and general language.

As a result of reading *Oh No! Not Another Problem* and practicing the process of *operational analysis,* you will improve your ability to:

- screen out emotional language and build a bridge to objectivity that will help you move beyond personal feelings and biased opinions.

- define problems and causes and not be misled by their symptoms.

- achieve greater control over yourself, circumstances, and individuals with whom you communicate.

- make a quick decision with minimal information when you don't have the time to gather all of the data.

Summary of Stories

The six stories in this book illustrate how different people apply the process of *operational analysis* as outlined in **The Ten-Step Guide to Analyze and Solve Problems** (Refer to page 5).

In the first story you meet George. He applies *operational analysis* to gather objective data to prove that the complaint filed against him and his dog is wrong. In researching his problem he takes the risk that he may discover his dog's barking is a nuisance.

The second story involves Barbara and Gary who look forward to enjoying a well-planned retirement. Two major unexpected events occur that cause them to reconsider their retirement plans. The story shows how flexible they are: ready to modify ideas and use change to their advantage.

Elaine, a woman looking for her ideal man, is the subject of the third story. In the process of analyzing the attributes she wants in a man, she tends to substitute one vague (non-operational) term for another. She becomes aware she is resistant to measurable data because it may challenge her judgment. The data may force her into reality and out of her comfortable emotional fantasy.

"I want – you provide" is the basis of the fourth story. Mike an eleven-year-old asks his parents for a horse. Mike's request gives his parents an opportunity to teach their son that saying "I want" is not enough to have his request accepted. He needs to back up his "I want" with factual information.

The fifth story introduces you to Scott, Branch Manager of an independent bank. A larger financial institution acquires the bank and establishes new policies and procedures, which reduce Scott's financial authority.   Scott must define and evaluate his position to determine whether he should stay in the bank or "quit."

The sixth story is about Susan, a woman whose husband dies suddenly. While she is still in a state of shock and disbelief, she finds herself jolted into dealing with the business and personal financial problems her husband and his partner had kept from her. She is compelled to make a quick decision without knowing what caused the problem.

All of the stories, characters and numerical data in this book are fictitious. Any resemblance to actual persons, living or dead, is purely coincidental.

Ten-Step Guide to Analyze and Solve Problems

The ten steps in the guide will help you apply the process of *operational analysis* (the organized collection of facts which reveals the measurable dimensions of problems that are described in vague and general language) to identify the real problem and its cause.

As you follow each step, you will become aware the data you seek in a particular step may not be found in that step but at a later point. The order of the steps is flexible to accommodate the various complications you may encounter in different problems.

Step 1: Recognize That A Problem May Exist.

- You may receive a written or oral complaint from an individual. You may observe that you are not satisfied with personal standards you have set. You may have to explain your "wants" to someone who selects what action to take. You may experience a series of unexpected events that cause you to question present or future plans.

- A problem can involve people, procedures, or systems.

Step 2: *Analyze The Background Material And Write A Statement Of The Problem.*

- Conduct a systematic search of all available background material related to the problem, facts and opinions.

- Review the information and separate facts from opinions. The more facts you have, the more operational (measurable) your initial problem statement will be.

- Write a statement of the problem, even if you use adjectives, adverbs and common nouns, which are vague and general (non-operational).

- Identify and/or list the vague and general (non-operational) terms in your written problem statement.

Step 3:   ***Gather The Data To Identify And Prove A Problem Exists.***

- Ask the questions **(who, what, when, where, how, why** and **costs)** that will reveal the facts of the problem statement in operational (measurable) terms.

- Use the collected data to determine the measurable difference (deviation) between an event that *should have happened* (measurable standard) and the event that *actually happened.*

- If the deviation revealed by the process of *operational analysis* is considered significant as established by statistical standards, personal measurable standards, or other objective standards, you have identified and proved a problem exists.

- If you cannot determine the deviation at this time, continue to Step 4.

Step 4:   *Gather Additional Data.*

- Refine the previous data you have collected and integrate it with the **NEW** data. Does the combined data now reveal what caused the deviation to occur?   If not, continue to Steps 5 and 6 to search for the cause of the deviation.

- You may discover data that you will use to establish options later in Steps 7 through 10.

- Additional data may reveal that there are multiple problems.   If other problems emerge, do not try to solve them unless they are a **part of the primary problem.**

Step 5:   *Review and Summarize The Collected Data*

- Examine all of the data you have been able to collect and analyze. Make a list of any data that is missing or non-operational. Operationally define the information (*determine the time, money, and resources required to collect the information.*)

- Do the results of the summary reveal a pattern or trend, expected or unexpected?

- It is vital the data and other information you have collected is complete and accurate or you will mistake the symptoms of a problem for the cause. Your solutions will be wrong and you or someone else will take an incorrect action to solve the problem. Worse, the problem will return.

Step 6:   *Evaluate The Data.*

- The cause of the problem may become evident in this step.

- Does the summary of the data indicate you have operationally defined the real problem and its cause in precise and measurable terms?

- Does the problem have to be redefined? If so, return to Step 3.

- The evaluation of the data collected on the cause of a problem may reveal unexpected results. You need to be flexible and receptive to what the data reveals to be the **real problem** and its cause. Avoid the tendency to hold on to preconceived ideas about what the data should reveal.

- If you (or someone else) want to determine only the real problem and its cause and not be concerned with solutions, stop now.

Step 7: *Write A Statement Of The Possible Action That Could Be Taken To Solve The Problem Before You Develop Criteria And Options.*

- The action you have to take may be the result of your analysis or options which have been given to you by someone else.

Step 8: *State The Criteria That A Solution To The Problem Must Meet.*

- Before you develop options to solve the problem, you need to know the restraints any solution must observe: legal, financial, time, or other measurable limits.

Step 9:   *Develop Options To Solve The Problem.*

- Apply the process of *operational analysis* when you **develop, analyze, summarize,** and **evaluate** each option.

- The advantages and disadvantages of each option should also be stated in operational terms.

Step 10:   *Select A Preferred Option To Solve The Problem.*

- Choose the option that meets your criteria and solves the problem.

- The option must have maximum financial, legal, and/or social benefits for you.

"I do not bark all the time."

The Barking Dog:
Keep It Quiet Or Lose It

George, a paralegal specializing in domestic law for a private law firm, has had a rough day interviewing clients. He's spent hours plowing through the emotions of angry and distraught couples to get to the facts of their cases.

Now, at the end of the day, he feels completely drained. He leaves the office later than usual, anticipating a relaxing evening with his dog and a good book. Traffic on the expressway is backed up due to an accident in the fast lane. For two hours George sits in his car listening to frustrated drivers honking their car horns and venting their feelings on the drivers around them. When George finally arrives home, he finds a letter taped to his front door from the Board of Directors of his Condominium Association. (See Figure 1-1)

Figure 1-1
Letter from Cascade View
Condominium Association
Board of Directors

September 21, 2000

Mr. George M.
Cascade View Condominium
Unit 18
Riverton, Maryland 20706

Dear Mr. M.:

The Board of Directors of Cascade View Condominiums has received a complaint from Tenant "A" stating that your dog barks all the time and this is disturbing him.

Please restrain the barking of your dog, Curio. We recommend you keep your kitchen window closed to help reduce the sound of the barking. You may also wish to consider taking your dog to obedience school.

You have 10 days in which to correct the situation. If no action is taken within this time period, the Board will declare your dog a nuisance in accordance with Article XXX of the CC&R's (Covenants, Conditions & Restrictions). The dog will then have to be removed from the condominium.

Please do not contact Tenant "A."

Sincerely,

Cascade View Condominium Association
Board of Directors

George's first reaction is, "I can't believe it. They won't dare. Curio doesn't bark that much. Just because my new neighbor doesn't like the dog doesn't mean the Board can throw her out! He's the one who should go!"

Although George is accustomed to separating facts from emotions in his professional life, his angry response to the Board's threat to separate him from his dog is understandable. George realizes he needs to redirect his energy and examine the situation objectively. To do this he uses the process of *operational analysis* as described in the ***Ten-Step Guide to Analyze and Solve Problems.*** (Refer to page 5)

Step 1, George **recognizes that a problem may exist.** In this case, the letter from the Cascade View Condominium Association Board of Directors indicates that a problem may exist.

Step 2, analyze the background material and write a statement of the problem. George's background material is the letter from the Condominium Association's Board of Directors. Since the letter refers to Article XXX of the CC&R's (Covenants, Conditions & Restrictions) as written in the Condominium's Bylaws, he reviews Article XXX.

While reading Article XXX George discovers *"only an owner can file a complaint."* Tenant "A" is a renter. Therefore, the letter issued by the Board is not valid. At this point, he experiences a rush of both positive and negative feelings. Since the Board's action is in error, he feels the exhilaration of "I got you." At the same time, he is angry with everyone on the Board for wasting his time and energy on a situation he believes is petty. Once again, emotions take the place of objectivity.

George works himself up to the point of calling every Board Member to "straighten them out." After he makes the phone calls pointing out the Board's mistake, George feels better. *He still has not proved whether a real problem exists.* George does not have enough information to answer the complaint about his barking dog. George has discovered only that the Board acted in violation of the CC&R's.

The next day the President of the Board of Directors leaves a message on George's answering machine notifying him the Board is going to reissue the notice with an OWNER'S complaint on behalf of Tenant "A" in accordance with Article XXX.

Faced with the Board's decision to pursue the complaint, George decides that allowing his emotions to run away with him is not going to solve the problem. Once again, he channels his emotions and focuses on the objective process of *operational analysis* (fact-finding).

The new letter from the Condominium Association's Board of Directors appears to be understandable. However, it contains general and vague language. George writes a statement of the problem.

- *A complaint from Owner "A" states, "your dog barks all the time and this is disturbing his tenant."*

The statement does not contain enough measurable information to identify the problem. To get the information George begins to list all the vague (non-operational) terms in the problem statement.

1. complaint

2. dog

3. barks

4. all the time

5. disturbing his tenant

He continues to **Step 3, gather data to identify and prove a problem exists.** He asks questions **(who, what, when, where, how, why and costs)** about each vague (non-operational) term. The answers to the following questions will help George identify the missing measurable information.

1. *Complaint*:

    Was the complaint oral or written? If it was oral, the statement may have changed in the communication from Owner "A" to the Board of Directors to George. If it was written, all George saw was one sentence that pertained to the problem. Other information may have been omitted.

2. *Dog:*

    What breed of dog? Age? Size? George knows he has a six-year-old female Shetland Sheepdog who weighs 23 pounds and stands 18 inches high. What he doesn't know is whether Curio is a suitable breed for condominium living.

3. *Barks:*

What does bark mean? Is it a harsh or sharp cry or some other sound? What is the intensity level of the noise?

4. *All the time:*

When? Both day and night? For how long?

5. *Disturbing his tenant:*

How? He can't sleep? Can't hear conversations? The noise overrides the volume on his television?

George continues to search for data that will operationally define the terms listed above. He proceeds to:

- Contact the County Public Safety Department and request a copy of their Dog Noise Ordinance.

- Review the minutes of the Board meetings to see whether any letters or comments about the dog's excessive barking were made by any other owners or tenants in the 52-unit condominium complex.

- Obtain a recognized standard regarding the suitability of a Shetland Sheepdog for condominium living.

- Interview ten of the nearest neighbors on his floor to ask if Curio's barking disturbs them.

A summary of the information reveals:

FACTS:

a. The County's Dog Noise Ordinance, Section 5, Article 2, defines its legal standard for "excessive noise" which constitutes a nuisance to mean barking, whining, howling and/or similar dog noise that lasts a minimum of ten minutes within an hour for two or more consecutive hours.

b. The Condominium Board did not reference any numerical standard for excessive noise.

c. The condominium records show, in the four years George has lived there, no complaints by owners or tenants have ever been filed about Curio's barking.

d. A nationally recognized dog breeders' association lists the Shetland Sheepdog fifth among the top ten breeds suitable for apartment living.

OPINIONS:

a. The neighbors on either side of George say the barking is not a problem to them.

b. Four people on George's floor comment that every day Tenant "A" leaves for work between 10:00 a.m. and 10:30 a.m. On his way to the elevator he stops outside George's kitchen window and teases Curio by making "meowing" cat sounds while running his fingers across the kitchen window screen. He also talks to the dog and threatens to hurt her. These actions cause the dog to bark.

c. George was unable to operationally define "disturbing him" because the Board of Directors stated George was not allowed to contact the complainant.

Having gathered the facts and opinions, George separates the information that is measurable and proven from that which is not relevant at this time. The County's Dog Noise Ordinance provides George with an objective and measurable standard of what constitutes a nuisance.

He proceeds to **Step 4, gather additional data.** George believes his dog does not bark "that much." The complaint states his dog barks, "all the time."

To prove or disprove whether his dog barks "all the time," he needs to find a method to measure the dog's barking habits. He uses a 24-hour digital recorder with a timer.

George continues to **Step 5, review and summarize the data** collected from the audio recordings. (See Figure 1-2)

Figure 1-2
Curio's Barking Habits
Summary of Audio Recordings
Monday – Friday

---

1. One-half minute every day between 6:55 a.m. and 7:05 a.m. when George gets ready to walk the dog.

2. Five seconds at 7:45 a.m. when George leaves for work.

3. One and one-half minutes between 10:00 a.m. and 10:15 a.m. Monday through Friday when Tenant "A" stops by the kitchen window and makes "meowing" cat sounds while running his fingers across the window screen. He also talks to the dog and threatens to hurt her.

4. Six seconds when the dog walker enters the condominium at 12:00 noon.

5. Five seconds when the dog walker leaves the condominium between 12:30 p.m. and 12:35 p.m.

6. One-half minute at 4:00 p.m. on Monday, four

seconds at 5:20 p.m.; Tuesday, two seconds at 3:15 p.m. and two seconds at 5:00 p.m.; Wednesday, one second at 3:20 p.m. and one second at 5:05 p.m.; Thursday, three seconds at 3:21 p.m. and one second at 5:07 p.m.; Friday, one-half minute at 4:03 p.m., three seconds at 5:02 p.m.

7. Four and one-half seconds each day when George comes home between 6:30 p.m. and 6:55 p.m.

8. Fifteen seconds when George takes the dog for a walk between 6:40 p.m. and 6:55 p.m.

9. One second when George comes back with the dog between 7:00 p.m. and 7:20 p.m.

10. When George is home there was no barking between 7:20 p.m. and 6:55 a.m. Monday, Tuesday, and Friday. Six seconds at 8:00 p.m. on Wednesday when George went out and one-half second when he returned at 11:30 p.m. No barking after that until 6:50 a.m. Thursday. Two seconds at 9:00 p.m. and one second at 9:45 p.m. on Thursday. No barking after that until one-half minute at 7:00 a.m. on Friday.

Step 6, an evaluation of the data reveals that the maximum per hour length of continuous barking and other dog noises made by his dog is one and one-half minutes in duration and occurs between 10:00 a.m. and 10:30 a.m. Monday through Friday when Tenant "A" stops by the kitchen window and teases the dog. The measurable difference between the County's ten-minute standard (what should happen) for excessive noise and Curio's barking time (what does happen) is eight and one-half minutes. Therefore, the dog cannot be legally considered a nuisance. *George has proven that his dog does not "bark all the time;" a problem does not exist.*

In a reply to the complaint, George presents his written research, audio recordings and a summary of all the results of his investigation to the Condominium's Board of Directors.

The Board of Directors reviews George's written report and listens to the recorded data with the owner who made the complaint. Based on the objective data the complaint is withdrawn and the owner informs his tenant that if he continues to harass the dog, he will be subject to eviction.

To avoid similar situations that George and other owners may encounter in the future, George submits three suggestions for procedural changes to Article XXX of the CC&R's. He asks the Cascade

View Condominium Association Board of Directors to present these changes to the homeowners for their consideration at their next general meeting which is being held in four weeks.

1. Include the County's legal standard for what dog noises constitute a nuisance.

2. Complaints of an infraction must be submitted in writing to the Board of Directors with proof of the infraction before the Board takes action.

3. The complainant will be held liable for all out-of-pocket expenses if he or she does not prevail in the opinion of the Board of Directors.

4. After ten days from the issuance of a letter of complaint, if no action to resolve the situation has been taken, the Board of Directors can then issue a summons to all owners named in the complaint. At that time all parties must appear before the Board Members to resolve the problem before further action can be taken.

As a result of George's objective research, the homeowners approved his suggestions for the procedural changes to Article XXX of the CC&R's. In addition, the homeowners requested that the Board of Directors review the CC&R's pertaining to other types of complaints to determine if they are measurably defined.

"Now, there's just the two of us."

Barbara and Gary: Retirement, A New Start

Barbara and Gary have carefully planned for their retirement. A major portion of their strategy centers on increasing their retirement income. To help make this possible Barbara, at age thirty-five, went to work for an apparel-manufacturing firm that had an excellent benefit plan. Throughout the years, Barbara advanced from Receptionist to her present position as Staff Assistant to the company's President.

For the past thirty-nine years Gary has been working for a plumbing and hardware supply company. He began on the assembly line, worked his way up to supervisor of Quality Assurance and now, at age sixty-five, is the department head of the Plumbing Division. Since Gary's company doesn't have an age sixty-five mandatory retirement policy, he is continuing to work until Barbara retires in four months at which time she will be age sixty-two.

All of their plans were on schedule until three months ago when two unexpected changes, both physical and emotional, occurred. Barbara's mother, who had lived with them for twenty years, died. Their youngest child was transferred by her company to Chicago.

Barbara and Gary realize they are no longer responsible for anyone but themselves. With all three of their children living out-of-state their four-bedroom home now seems too large. The combination of these events leads them to think about the possibility of selling their home. They contact a realtor who has approached them several times during the past year. She meets with them and explains they can probably get $700,000 if they sell now.

They are astounded! When they purchased their home 30 years ago they paid just $24,500. In recent years the homes in their area on Long Island have been selling for $325,000. Now that amount has more than doubled. The prospect of this surprising windfall leads them to *raise the question* of whether they should consider alternatives to their present retirement plan. **They recognize a problem may exist. Step 1.**

Barbara and Gary continue to **Step 2, analyze the background material and write a statement of the problem.** They call other realtors to verify if what they had been told about the state of the housing market in their area is correct. Yes, there is a shortage of homes for sale in the area and the realtor is correct; they can expect a minimum of $680,000 and a possible maximum of $725,000. They contact their accountant to obtain an estimate of how much Federal and State Income tax they will have to pay if they sell their home.

After discussing and organizing all of the facts and opinions they gathered, Barbara and Gary write a general statement of their problem.

- *Should we continue with our present retirement plans or should we make some changes?*

Barbara and Gary proceed to **Step 3, gather data to identify and prove a problem exists.** There are two separate thoughts in their statement that need to be analyzed. One, should we continue with our present retirement plan? Two, should we make some changes? Barbara and Gary start their analysis with the first thought in the problem statement. They begin with a review of the outline of their present financial and retirement activity plans.

Summary of Financial Retirement Plan

1. Combined yearly income amounts to $44,232 (pensions, social security, interest on two $10,000 C.D.'s and a 401K plan).

2. Expenses will total $23,744 per year (health, life and car insurance, living expenses such as food and clothing, etc., property taxes, maintenance of the house including utilities if they continue to live in their present home, which is mortgage free).

3. $1,100 per month for savings, travel and other expenses after Federal and State Income taxes are paid.

Activity Plans

The second part of their original retirement plan centers on what Barbara and Gary will do with their time after retiring. They would like to:

1. Increase their computer knowledge.

2. Spend more time with friends.

3. Travel out of state to visit their children and grandchild.

4. Take trips to see other parts of the country.

5. Resume community activities.

6. Increase the amount of time spent on maintaining health which includes playing more golf.

While they have described their financial plans in precise terms, they have used vague and general (non-operational) language to describe their activity plans. To avoid any misunderstandings and clarify their ideas, they begin to operationally define the dimensions of their activities **(who, what, when, where, how, why and costs)** by asking questions:

1. What does increase our computer knowledge mean? Program design? What programs? Application in what areas? Use our present computer or upgrade to a new one? What are the costs?

2. How much time do we want to spend with friends? Together or separately?

3. How long will we spend with each of our children? When? What are the costs?

4. How many trips do we want to take? How long will we stay? What do we mean by see other parts of the country? What are the costs?

5. Resume what types of activities in the community? Volunteer work? How much time will we spend on these unnamed activities? What will it cost to join a service club?

6. Increase by how much the amount of time we will spend maintaining our good health. Join a health club? Go to a community fitness center? How much time will we spend playing golf? What are the costs?

As a result of answering these and other questions, Barbara and Gary discover they have different ideas about what they want to do and how much time and money will be required. Barbara wants to increase her knowledge of accounting. She may want to enroll in a series of computer accounting courses offered at a senior center. Gary wants to buy a new computer so he can take advantage of the new technology and expand his range of knowledge. When trying to determine the amount of time they will spend with others, they find they have not considered any future plans their family and friends may have scheduled. Although they cannot measurably define all of the questions related to their activity plans, the process of *operational analysis* does enable them to measure and clarify all but questions 2 and 3, which may have no significant meaning at this time.

Barbara and Gary proceed to operationally define what they mean in the second part of their problem statement, "should we make some changes?" They consider three changes they may make if they sell their house.

A. Buy a smaller home in the same area. Pay cash and invest the balance of the money.

B. Move out-of-state, possibly outside of Tampa, Florida. Two years ago they spent ten days in the area visiting friends who had moved to a gated community. They liked their friends' townhouse which is situated on a golf course.

C. Purchase a Recreational Vehicle (RV) and spend a year or so traveling around the country.

Barbara and Gary continue to **Step 4, gather additional data** to determine whether there is a significant financial difference between what should happen if they retain their present retirement plan and then compare it with what could happen if they make a change. They apply the process of *operational analysis* to develop, analyze, summarize and evaluate each change.

They begin with change A. Barbara and Gary ask the realtor to set-up appointments to look at various townhouses, smaller patio homes and condominiums. They find one patio home for $525,000 and one townhouse for $450,000, each within a 10-mile radius of their present location. After looking at what property is available in their area, they decide to test the market for 90 days and list their home at an asking price of $725,000.

Before exploring change B, Barbara and Gary review their health insurance and find it is transferable to medical services in Florida. They ask their friends to contact the Chamber of Commerce, and the nearby university to send them brochures and information about various activities in the community. They combine this information with materials they obtain from the Internet. Finally they make arrangements to visit their friends in Florida to evaluate the cost of housing and living conditions.

Gary proceeds to change C and calls another friend who puts him in contact with a RV dealer who tells him a mid-range motor home will cost approximately $68,000. A small, used car to pull behind the RV will cost approximately $14,000. Barbara and Gary's present automobile is too big for the motor home to pull. The cost of insurance, campsite rentals, gasoline, utilities and the necessary equipment to pull a car will have to be investigated. There will also be the cost of packing and storing their home furnishings.

They continue to **Step 5, review and summarize the collected data**, which they have gathered to this point. While they review the data, the realtor contacts them with a written offer for their house and a deposit for a sale price of $725,000. The prospective buyer is being transferred from out-of-state and wants a 120-day escrow. After paying real estate broker commissions, escrow fees, capital gains and other local taxes they will net $638,000 in cash.

If they retain their present retirement plan and do not sell the house they will have no additional income. If they accept the offer to sell their house for $725,000 they will have $638,000 in cash to invest. There will be a significant deviation of 100%.

Barbara and Gary have proved a problem exists. The cause of the deviation is the over 300% plus increase in property values over a period of thirty years.

They continue to **Step 6, evaluate the data.** The offer accelerates the decision-making process. Barbara and Gary conclude the most practical financial action to take is to sell their house, especially with the favorable terms of the offer. They answer their original question, whether to continue with their present retirement plans or make some changes. *They will make a change in their present retirement plans.*

Barbara and Gary proceed to **Step 7, write a statement of the possible action that could be taken to solve the problem before you develop criteria and options.**

- *Which change, A, B or C shall we choose that will meet our financial and emotional needs?*

Before Barbara and Gary can decide what change to choose, they have to **state the criteria that a solution to the problem must meet, Step 8.** They establish a minimum financial criterion of $1,000 a month increase in their retirement income.

Barbara and Gary proceed to **Step 9, analyze the options.** They elect to use changes A, B, and C as their options. They begin with option C. After they gather additional information, including *dollarizing* the hidden costs of full-time RV travel, they decide to eliminate option C. At first, full-time living in a RV sounded like fun. However, further investigation proves this is not the lifestyle they want for themselves.

Barbara and Gary continue to gather additional data on the financial implications of option A. They had seen a two-bedroom townhouse in their area for $450,000. Following the sale of their home, and the purchase of the townhouse, they will net $188,000 cash. If the cash is invested at 5%, they will increase their monthly retirement income of $1,100 by an estimated $783 per month which does not meet their financial criteria. They reject option A.

A review of the data on the financial benefits of option B, as a choice, appears more positive. On a weekend trip to Florida they find a 2-bedroom townhouse that will be available when they are ready to relocate. It is in a complex five blocks from their friends. The cost is $215,000 with a current monthly maintenance fee of $175 per month. After purchasing the townhouse, they will net $423,000. To cover the cost of moving, buying new furniture and any other incurred expenses, they will reserve $70,000, leaving them with a balance of $353,000 to invest. If they invest this amount at a minimum of

5% interest, it will increase their monthly retirement income of $1,100 by $1,470 a month. The increase will give them a total of $2,570 a month. Option B meets their financial criteria.

Other financial benefits of living in Florida include an estimated 30% decrease in cost-of-living expenses and no State Income Tax. They will need to reside in Florida for a year to determine how much additional monthly income these benefits will provide.

There are also non-financial incentives for the couple's move. The warm climate will allow them more time to devote to their outdoor activities. Barbara and Gary are tired of coping with the increased traffic and crowded stores in their Long Island community. The move to a less congested locale is an inviting alternative.

Before making their final decision, they also consider the emotional impact of the move to Florida, leaving friends and long-time relationships with doctors, bankers and others who make life enjoyable, safe and comfortable. However, they have their friends of 20 years in Florida who will introduce them to professional resources in the area.

They proceed to **Step 10, select a preferred option to solve the problem.** Based on all of the data and information they have, *Barbara and Gary choose option B, to move to Florida.*

Barbara and Gary look forward to a new start. Because they applied the process of *operational analysis* to all three options, they will be less likely to question their final decision. Second guessing of "if only" we had made a different choice will be avoided. Once they are settled in Florida if they encounter unexpected problems or differences in their financial or activity plans, Barbara and Gary will use the process of *operational analysis* to attempt to resolve them.

"Your condo is worth how much?"

Elaine:
36, Single and Looking

Elaine is a 36-year-old stockbroker living in Seattle, Washington. Three years ago she met what she thought was her "ideal man." The relationship lasted only two months before she broke up with him. *"Something was missing!"* Despite the fact she dates approximately three times a month she still has not found a man with whom she would like to have a long-term relationship. Again, *"something always seems to be missing,"* even when she feels the chemistry is right. She recognizes **Step 1, that a problem may exist.**

Elaine proceeds to **Step 2, analyze background material and write a statement of the problem.** Elaine finds her situation frustrating because she has what she believes is a clear picture in her mind of the type of man she wants. To investigate and analyze her problem, Elaine converts her mental image of her ideal man into written form.

"I want a man who has at least as much as I have. Someone who is good-looking, healthy, fun, interesting and educated. A man who has a future, and is not too young or too old. Someone who is single, but interested in getting married. He lives locally, is nice, considerate and emotionally stable."

The statement is open to a variety of interpretations. It contains vague and general (non-operational) language. Elaine does not know what the attribute good-looking means. How young is young? To clarify her thoughts she rewrites her initial statement of the type of man she wants.

"The man I want has to own a car, real estate and earn a good living. He should be attractive and tall, have a firm body, and be interested in taking care of himself. A man who has an education. He has to have a sense of humor and the ability to communicate. He must be chemically free. He has to show common sense, be understanding, and be willing to learn. He has to be thoughtful. He has to be mature, be a professional or own a business. He should be around my age and definitely be free of any obligations from a previous marriage or relationship. Someone who lives nearby."

Although Elaine is attempting to be more specific in her second statement, she is merely substituting one vague term for another. Once again, she words the statement in general terms. The description consists of emotional words, adjectives, adverbs, and general nouns, not measurable facts. For the phrase "good-looking" she substitutes "tall, has a firm body." She replaces "not too young or too old" with "around my age." Given the wording of her first and second statement, she still cannot determine what the attributes mean. She reviews the background material and writes a general statement of the problem:

- *I want a long-term relationship but there is always "something missing" in the men I date.*

Elaine proceeds to **Step 3, gather data to identify and prove a problem exists**. Before she can have a long-term relationship, Elaine must first determine what she means by *something is missing*. She asks questions about each attribute she describes in vague terms. The answers will reveal the measurable dimensions of the attributes **(who, what, where, when, how, why and costs)**. (See Figure 3-1)

Figure 3-1
Attributes
Questions and Answers

---

1. Q. What type of car must he have?
    A. Own a standard American luxury car that costs over $40,000.

2. Q. What type of real estate (income or residential) and what is the financial value of the real estate?
    A. Own his own home, not a condo, which costs over $300,000.

3. Q. How much money does he have to earn?
    A. Six figures per year.

4. Q. How tall should he be? Weight? How does he maintain a "firm" body?
    A. At least 5'10" tall but not over 6'2". Weight around 160 pounds depending on his height. Exercises either at home or at a gym.

5. Q. What type of humor? How do I define ability to communicate?
    A. Has a dry sense of humor. Initiates conversation without having to be prompted.

6. Q. How much education?
   A. Four or more years of college.

7. Q. What do I mean by "common sense and needs to be willing to learn?"
   A. Needs to be practical in everyday matters. Seeks knowledge about a variety of subjects, such as science and theater.

8. Q. What type of profession? What type of business?
   A. Is in a professional position outside of the financial or legal fields. A successful business owner whose profits will increase by 20% within the next ten years.

9. Q. What is "not too young or too old?"
   A. Two years younger or seven years older than me.

10. Q. What do I mean by, "no obligations from a previous marriage or relationship?"
    A. No financial responsibility to an ex-wife or girl friend.

11. Q. How close is nearby?
    A. Within a two-hour radius of Seattle .

12. Q. How do I define thoughtful and understanding?
    A. Considerate of my feelings. Shows good judgment

13. Q. Chemically free? Drugs? Alcohol?
    A. Not addicted to any prescription medications or drugs. Moderate drinker (4 one ounce drinks per week). A non-smoker.

The answers give Elaine measurable standards for 77% of the attributes. To prove a problem exists, first she selects nine of the measured attributes which she will use as a standard for what her ideal man should have.

1. Chemically free.

2. Financial value of real estate.

3. Type and cost of automobile.

4. Earnings.

5. Professional career.

6. Marital status.

7. Appearance, height and weight.

8. Age.

9. Educational background.

Elaine then compares these operationally defined attributes (what he should have) with the actual attributes (what he did have) of ten of the men she dated two or more times during the last three years. (See Figure 3-2)

Figure 3-2
Results of Attribute Comparison

1. Seven were chemically free.

2. Only one owned a home valued over $300,000. Three owned condo's under $250,000. All had mortgages of an unknown amount. Six rented apartments.

3. Four drove an American luxury car that cost over $40,000. Six drove foreign-made automobiles which cost under $40,000.

4. Five earned six figures or over a year and five earned between $60,000 and $85,000.

5. Three were in professions outside the financial and legal fields; two were in real estate and five were non-professionals. None owned his own business.

6. Four had been divorced and had children, six had never been married.

7. Seven were between 5'10" and 6' tall and three were between 6'4" and 6'5" and six of the ten were overweight.

8. Four were her age, two were seven years younger and four were ten to fifteen years older.

9. Four were college graduates; three had a degree in business; one had a degree in computer science; two had no degree.

The outcome of the comparison reveals none of the ten men have all nine measurable attributes. There is a significant deviation of 100%. Elaine has identified and proved a problem exists. However, she does not know the cause of the problem. Is it the standards she has established for the attributes? Are they based on facts or fantasy? Does the fact she wants her "ideal" man to have all nine of the measurable attributes impact on the deviation?

To discover answers to these questions, she proceeds to **Step 4, gather additional data** on each attribute and its measurable standard. She begins with the financial standards that are based on her criteria, "he must have at least as much as I have." The facts are: she owns a condo not a home with a value of $340,000. She drives a foreign not an American car which costs $55,000. The combined data reveals to Elaine she has set two financial standards that contradict her criteria. Based on that information she realizes it is impossible for the men she dates to have all nine of the measurable attributes. She has identified three standards which are the major causes for the unexpected deviation of 100%.

As a result of the data, Elaine revises her financial standards to meet her criteria. He must have a minimum of $700,000 in combined financial assets which can now include real estate (condo or house) automobile (foreign or domestic), a retirement plan, cash or other investments.

From her original list of nine measurable attributes, she selects three additional attributes he must have: earn at least $125,000 per year; have four or more years of college and be chemically free. Elaine has now narrowed down to four the number of attributes and their measurable standards.

She places the measurable attributes of marital status, appearance, profession and age on a priority level of "would like to have" rather than "must have."

Elaine continues to **Step 5, review and summarize the collected data.** Elaine examines her question-and-answer list of attributes to determine whether information is missing or has not been operationally defined.

She starts to review the attributes and discovers she has mixed the non-operational attributes, practical with willing to learn; thoughtful with understanding; sense of humor with the ability to communicate. She separates them and selects two of the attributes her ideal man must have: ability to communicate and dry sense of humor. In the past Elaine relied on her intuition and immediate impression as her standard for the non-operational attributes. She decides to test her reasoning and begins with an analysis of these two attributes.

Elaine's non-operational standard of the attribute "ability to communicate" is a man who will initiate a conversation without having to be prompted. To establish a measurable standard she asks questions to clarify what she means by the term conversation. Is it content? If so, on what subjects? World events? Sports? Art? Business? A variety of topics or only specific topics? She decides her measurable standard (what should happen), is that he will have to initiate a conversation on any subject 50% of the time. To determine what actually happens, she will gather data as the result of the conversations she has with her future dates. If the deviation is significant, she will determine whether she has to change or modify her measurable standards.

She continues to the second non-operational attribute her "ideal" man must have, a dry sense of humor. Elaine's standard for a dry sense of humor is intellectual wit rather than loud or coarse humor. She wants a man who can contrast or combine ideas and express them in a word or phrase quickly and with humor. Her measurable standard for the attribute (what should happen) is he must not express loud or coarse humor more than 5% of the time. To determine what actually happens, she will count the number of times her date expresses that type of humor. Any deviation will not be acceptable to her.

Further review of the data indicates to Elaine that she has not operationally defined what she means by the statement, "she is looking for a man with whom she would like to have a long-term relationship."

How long? Six months? A year? What does she mean by the word relationship? Live together? Maintain separate living facilities? Marriage? Data is missing. Elaine operationally defines these terms: long-term is a minimum of one year; maintain separate living facilities and no consideration of marriage for at least two years.

Elaine **evaluates the data, Step 6.** The data reveals the original cause of the problem is not what is missing in the men she dates, but is with Elaine's vague description of her "ideal" man. After she operationally defines the attributes, she finds the real cause of her problem is due to the false financial standards she set and the absolute requirement he must meet all of her measurable standards.

Through the process of *operational analysis,* Elaine now has ***new measurable standards*** for six of the most important attributes her "realistic" man must have. She wants to find a man who: wants a relationship for a minimum of one year, will maintain separate living facilities and doesn't want to consider marriage for at least two years. He must have a minimum of $700,000 in combined financial assets which can include real estate (condo or house), automobile (foreign or domestic), a retirement plan, cash or other investments. He has to earn at least $125,00 per year, have four or more years of college and not be addicted to any prescription medications or drugs. A moderate drinker (4 one-ounce drinks per week). A non-smoker. A man who can initiate a conversation on any subject 50% of the time. A man who has an intellectual wit, who can contrast or combine ideas and express them quickly and with humor. He cannot express loud or coarse humor more than 5% of the time.

As she continues to date, she will compare over time the six measurable attributes she wants her "realistic" man to have with the actual attributes of her dates to determine differences and their significance. She will have an objective process to help her make what will be one of the most important decisions of her life.

Of course, Elaine must answer the question, what measurable attributes does she have to attract the man she wants?

"You don't even take care of your dog."

Mike's Birthday Wish: "I Want, You Provide"

Mike will soon reach his eleventh birthday. He and his father, John, are about to go on a day's fishing excursion to celebrate. Mike is really excited.

John's position as Vice President of Sales for a Denver-based computer company requires him to travel at least two weeks a month. With a new marriage, family and job responsibility, he doesn't see his son as often as he likes. Despite these factors, Mike and his dad have a good relationship. Mike loves his dad and enjoys their time together. When they can't see each other, they communicate by e-mail and telephone.

On the drive to the lake, Mike and his father talk about his upcoming birthday and his special "wish" for a horse. Mike tells his dad all about his two best friends who own horses which they let him ride. But he wants a horse of his own. His friends know someone who wants to sell a fifteen-year-old American Quarterhorse for $500, and it will not cost very much a month to keep a horse at the house. Mike suggests instead of giving him extra money to attend special sports events, John can put it toward the upkeep of a horse.

John immediately asks if Mike has spoken to his mother about the horse. Mike hesitates and states that his mother has said "no" because she can't afford the extra expenses at this time. John recognizes that Mike may have a problem.

He asks Mike if he has considered the problems involved in owning a horse. If his idea is to keep the horse at his house, has he checked out the zoning laws? It could be his friends live in an area zoned for horses and he may not.

John continues to ask other questions. How does he plan to keep the horse sheltered in the winter? What is the cost of a saddle and tack? What is the price of feed? What additional expenses are involved? Is Mike prepared to take care of an animal on a daily basis, particularly since his mother is now feeding, cleaning and brushing the dog Mike "had to have?" Can he be relied upon to be responsible for the proper care and feeding of an animal which may have a life span of over twenty years?

Aside from a few "but Dad" interruptions, Mike is silent. After a few minutes, he tells his father he cannot answer his questions. Hearing the frustration in his son's voice, John tells Mike that he will explain a problem-solving process he can use to obtain the answers he needs. John suggests that if Mike will do the research and come up with precise answers to his questions and the exact costs involved in the purchase and maintenance of the horse, he will then speak to Mike's mother. Together they will give the matter serious consideration.

He tells Mike he thinks he is old enough to learn that if he is going to make a request involving a major financial investment, a general vague (non-operational) statement such as "I want a horse because my friends have one" is not a sufficient reason to justify the purchase. Mike needs to learn how to define and measure his wants and to consider how his desires may impact others. John will contact Mike's mother and explain their conversation. John tells Mike that if he has any questions while he is doing his research he can come to him or his mother for help.

The next day Mike begins his project. First, he shows his mother the list of questions his dad discussed with him. He asks his mother if she knows what the local zoning laws are for their property. She doesn't have the answers he needs. However, she finds a property description, which will enable him to get the correct information from the zoning department. He contacts the City's Planning Department and is told that his home is located in Zone 563, and it is permissible to keep up to three horses.

Mike, encouraged and excited, continues with the fact-finding phase of his problem by searching the Internet for information on horses. He also makes an appointment to go to two local stables after school so he can speak with the owners to obtain first-hand information. Mike needs answers to the following questions:

1. What breed of horse will be the best for his minimal experience?

   - An eight-year-old American Quarterhorse gelding, without papers.

2. What is the cost of the horse he should buy?

   - Costs range from $1,000 to $5,000 for an experienced horse.

   - A show horse could cost a minimum of $10,000.

3. What is the cost of a saddle?

   - New Tack-2 pads, saddle, bridle costs $500 to $1,000. Used $250. One-time costs.

4. What is the cost of the feed?

   - A horse of this breed should have 420 pounds of hay per month. The hay costs $47.14 per month. Also, the diet should include 3 pounds a day of 4-way general sweet mix grain. The grain costs $16.20 per month. The delivery charge is $25.00 per month. The total monthly cost of the feed including delivery is $88.34.

5. What type of winter shelter does the horse require?

   - A windbreak, a barn, shed or lean-to. Costs can range from $350 to $6,000, depending upon choice of shelter.

6. What additional costs are involved?

   - Yearly Vet Maintenance - $100, includes worming, shots for diseases. Injuries - office call at $50; treatment $50-$200 for cuts, lameness, infections. Fee to "put down" $350-$500.

   - Farrier Maintenance – horse-shoeing, $200 a year.

- A bucket of grooming supplies – heavy brush, hoof pick, currycomb and fly repellent, $100.

- Increase in homeowners liability insurance from $300,000 to $1,000,000 with a $1,000 deductible for bodily injury and property damage, $60.00 per year.

With his parents' guidance, Mike researches, gathers and reviews the facts. He finds the minimum initial cost of an 8-year old Quarterhorse, saddle, tack, and feed is $2600. The fifteen-year-old Quarterhorse his friends tell him he can buy for $500 is older than recommended for someone of his limited riding experience.

He still persists. Mike remembered one of the stable owners had suggested two other options which would allow him to board a horse at a location other than his house.

One option is to board the horse at a nearby stable. One of the advantages of a boarding stable environment is it enables horses to bond with other horses and small animals such as goats. This helps the horse to feel safe and not become lonely. A stall, pasture and feed will cost $175-$300 a month. Mike will not have to worry about the costs of buying and hauling the feed. He can ride and care for the horse every day. However, even if his parents buy the horse, he will still have the start-up costs of buying the needed equipment to maintain the animal.

Option two is to board the horse at a ranch. The pasture fee will cost $30-$95 per month. There are no stall care, feed or water charges. The horse will basically take care of itself. The person in charge will inspect the animal daily and brush it as time permits. However, the ranch is more remotely located than the stable. Transportation involves a 50-mile round-trip.

While investigating option two, Mike is told the liability insurance carried by a boarding ranch or stable will not allow his friends to ride their horses at either location. He believes he has wasted his time. Mike's mother understands his reaction and points out that before he developed options he should have asked first if his friends could bring their own horses and ride with him.

The reality of the costs proves to Mike that, at this time, it will be impossible for him to own a horse. He presents all of the facts to his parents in an organized manner. After a review of Mike's research, John suggests a long-term plan for him to consider. Mike can open a special savings account towards perhaps a 3-year goal to owning a horse. If Mike is serious and wants to show he has a sense of responsibility, he can deposit in the account the extra spending money he receives from John, his mother and/or relatives. As time goes on, he can make some extra money with small jobs around the area. Each year Mike and his parents will review his account to see if the length of time required for Mike to reach his goal has to be changed. Mike agrees to the plan.

John, once again, explains to Mike that the research he went through to arrive at the facts in his investigation is similar to the ***Ten-Step Guide to Analyze and Solve Problems*** (Refer to page 5) he uses at work before he presents management with a new idea or suggestion for change. Just like Mike, John begins by stating what he wants in vague terms. Then he gathers the facts necessary to put his ideas and words into operational (measurable) terms to determine whether the "I want" meets the capabilities and realistic limitations of management. John continues to explain that his use of problem analysis doesn't guarantee he will get what he wants. However, the process does increase the probability his ideas will be considered, just as he has reviewed Mike's proposal after he presented the results of his research.

As a consequence of Mike's investigation he is able to communicate with his parents in a more realistic and objective way. His parents are pleased that with guidance he took the time to complete his research. By doing so, Mike gained an understanding of how he could apply the process to his schoolwork: analyze exam questions; complete class assignments; evaluate research or essay papers. His parents will continue to reinforce this pattern of objective thinking so it will become an everyday part of his life.

"Sure wish I could help you Mr. Baker."

Scott's Decision:
Stay In The Job Or Quit

Ten years ago, Scott graduated from college with a BA in business and finance. At that time he applied for a position as a management trainee with a large commercial bank in the city of Ft. Worth, Texas. Entry into the program was on hold due to a six-month hiring freeze. The Director of Human Resources was impressed with Scott's academic record, his positive attitude, and his commitment to community service. He offered Scott a job in the interim as a teller.

At age twenty-three, after the freeze was lifted, Scott entered the program. During the next three years, he learned all aspects of operations, customer service, lending, facility management, and computer-related banking services. His last year as a trainee was spent at the bank's headquarters in Philadelphia, Pennsylvania. At the completion of the program he was offered a job with a 3% salary increase in the Advanced Planning Department at the bank's headquarters. Scott considered the offer. He explained to management his interest was in the personal aspect of banking rather than overall policies and procedures.   He was told the only available openings in customer relations were in the Philadelphia area. Scott wanted to return to Ft. Worth, where he was raised and educated. He missed the contact with his family and friends, as well as his involvement in community activities. He rejected the offer.

When he returned home, Scott found a position as Assistant Branch Manager at a small independent bank with six branches in the immediate Ft. Worth area. In the next four years the bank expanded and purchased another small bank, which brought the total number of branches to fifteen. Scott remained at his branch and was promoted to Branch Manager, a position he has held for the past two years. He enjoys the atmosphere of this suburban branch and is well-known for his participation in the community.

Recent rumors of a take-over by a larger bank with headquarters in New York prove to be true. Scott wonders how this take-over will affect his job and recognizes **Step 1, a problem may exist.**

Scott proceeds to **Step 2, analyze the background material and write a statement of the problem.** In a preliminary meeting with the new management team, Scott is told the bank wants him to stay in his current position. They outline the changes in his responsibilities as Branch Manager. Scott is concerned about the changes in his financial responsibilities and its impact on customer service. In addition, the branch manager's budget for support of community and local charity events will be reduced by approximately 45%, although the bank will meet its prior commitments.

At the next meeting, the Area Manager instructs the Branch Managers on the computer software programs, which explain the bank's new policies and procedures. They in turn are expected to train all of their employees. The Area Manager monitors the training process and observes Scott's communication and computer skills. He asks him to assist the managers who are having difficulty implementing the new programs. Scott continues to manage his branch office and spends two months, including evenings and weekends, on the assignment. For his extra effort, he receives neither a bonus nor an offer of one of the new positions created by the acquisition. Scott is discouraged and begins to doubt whether he has a future with the new bank. He writes a statement of the problem.

- *Do I stay in the new bank or do I quit?*

Figure 5-1
Comparison of Financial Responsibilities
Branch Manager Position

Responsibilities	Former Bank *(What Did Happen)*	New Bank *(What Now Happens)*
Lending authority (autos, home equity, line-of-credit)	Maximum of $700,000 per loan	None. Loans and Line-of-Credit referred to Main Branch Loan Department.
Overdraft Approval	Maximum of $10,000 per customer	None. Branch Manager to assist customer to establish a line-of-credit
Reversal of Bank Charges	Option of Manager	No option. Recommend with written justification, and send to Operations at Main Branch.

He continues to **Step 3, gather the data to identify and prove a problem exists.** Scott considers one of the most important aspects of the job is his authority to make financial decisions which benefit the customer. He begins to operationally define as many of the changes as possible (**who, what, when where, how, why and costs**) in his financial responsibilities listed in the new job description. (See Figure 5-1)

There is a significant deviation of 100% between Scott's former financial responsibilities as Branch Manager (what did happen) and the new financial responsibilities of the Branch Manager (what now happens), which proves a problem exists.

Scott continues to **Step 4, gather additional data.** Scott is concerned his redefined financial authority will limit his ability to provide the personalized service he has given his customers in the past. The customers are already complaining about the new policies and the bank's "uncaring" attitude toward their individual needs.

Before Scott can analyze the customer complaints, the District Manager informs him the current Area Manager is going to take early retirement in sixty days. He offers Scott the job based on his past performance and provides him with a copy of the job description which includes:

- Manage eight branch managers

- Guarantee branch managers are in compliance with bank regulations and laws related to their job

- Refer all loans to appropriate loan department

- Approve documented overdrafts up to $5,000 per customer and reverse bank fee charges up to $50 per account with written justification by branch manager

- Travel (per diem for gas and use of personal car) to other branches

- Be on call twenty-four hours for emergencies

The District Manager offers Scott $61,000 a year with annual stock options up to $1,500. His other current benefits remain the same. Scott has two weeks in which to accept or reject the job. If he rejects the offer, he can stay in his present position. He thanks the District Manager for considering him for the position and tells him he will have an answer for him within the specified time period.

While he has operationally defined the financial responsibilities of the new branch and area manager, Scott needs to determine the amount of time he will spend with his customers as Branch Manager versus as Area Manager. (See Figure 5-2)

Figure 5-2
Comparison of Time Spent with Customers

New Bank Branch Manager	New Bank Area Manager
30% on the phone with customers' complaints & inquiries.	0% on the phone with customers.
10% personal contact with customers.	1% personal contact with customers.

An analysis of the data reveals a 100% deviation between the time a branch manager will spend on the phone with customers and the time an area manager will spend on the phone with customers. There is a 99% deviation in face-to-face customer contact between the new branch manager and the area manager. Scott considers the deviations to be significant, and in conjunction with his financial analysis has proved a problem exists if he stays in the bank. The cause of the deviations is based on the policies of the new bank.

To define what it means to "quit," he needs to investigate the present job market. He searches the Internet for opportunities and contacts several organizations outside of the banking profession. Over the weekend, he discusses his situation with his fiancee, Melissa, a marketing manager for a computer software company. Scott shows her the data he has collected and expresses his disappointment with the overall changes at the bank.

As Melissa listens to Scott and looks over the information, she remembers hearing of an opening at CSI Software Company. The firm designs and manufactures products for financial institutions. She understands the Vice President of Public Relations is looking for an Assistant

Director of Community Relations who has established ties with the community and has experience with financial software. She thinks the job is worth investigating. Scott agrees and says he will call the vice president to request an interview for the position.

The Vice President of Public Relations at CSI Software returns his call and arranges an interview for the following day. Four days later, Scott is offered the position with a yearly salary of $63,000 and a hiring bonus of $2,500. As Assistant Director of Community Relations, he would be a spokesperson for CSI Software and would assume some of the vice president's speaking commitments. In addition, he would work with and train CSI's customers in the application of the company's product lines.

At first the job seems perfect. Scott thinks he wants to leave the bank and CSI Software appears to combine his interest in finance with civic activities. He needs more data before he can make a final decision whether to accept the offer. Scott has operationally defined what it means to stay as a branch or an area manager at the bank; but the ramifications of quitting are still vague (non-operational).

He phones the vice president to clarify the

vague (non-operational) statements made during the interview. You will:

- Travel

- Be telecommuting

- Attend some early meetings

- Work some evenings

- Go to conventions

The vice president gives Scott more specific information:

- Spend one week a month in the Dallas area.

- His at-home work hours may vary from five to twenty hours per week.

- At present there are four breakfast meetings per month.

- From September to January there are fifteen evening meetings and/or fundraisers with community organizations.

- Approximately one month per year is spent at conventions

Since the position has just been created, the specific number of hours spent on each activity has not yet been determined. The vice president tells Scott that unless there is a special meeting at the office he can establish his own working hours to coincide with his travel, presentations, training CSI customers, and meetings with new and previous contacts. He will be furnished with a laptop computer which he will use to telecommute from his home or on the road. Scott adds the information to his other data to operationally define what to expect if he "quits" the bank.

Scott continues to **Step 5, review and summarize the collected data.** He starts his review with data that relates to paid benefits. He makes a comparison between branch and area manager and assistant director of community relations at CSI Software. (See Figure 5-3) Scott realizes if he remains with the new bank as branch manager his salary will continue at $55,000 per year, without stock options. If he accepts the promotion to area manager, his salary will increase to $61,000 with stock options up to

Figure 5-3
Comparison of Paid Benefits

Branch Manager New Bank	Area Manager New Bank	Assistant Director of Community Relations CSI Software
$55,000 a year	$61,000 a year	$63,000 a year $2,500 Hiring Bonus
No stock options	Stock options, up to $1,500 a year	Stock options, up to $4,000 a year

$1,500 per year. If Scott accepts the job at CSI, his salary will increase to $63,000 per year with stock options up to $4,000 a year. He will receive a hiring bonus of $2,500. Scott then compares the difference in organizational benefits between the bank and CSI Software. (See Figure 5-4, page 80)

Scott proceeds to **Step 6, evaluate the data.** Aside from the increase in salary and benefits, CSI offers Scott the opportunity to be associated with a company on the cutting edge of computer technology and to continue his involvement with community service and charitable organizations.

The position at CSI Software is not as structured as the position at the bank. Scott will have the chance to define a minimum of 20% of his job based on his standards. In addition, he will report directly to the Vice President of Public Relations, which reduces the layers of management he will have to go through to get a decision.

He evaluates all the collected information, measurable and vague, and decides to "quit" the bank and accept the position at CSI Software.

Figure 5-4
Organizational Benefits
Difference Between New Bank and CSI Software

	New Bank	CSI Software
Health Benefits	50% paid	100% paid
Sick Leave	1 wk. after 60 dys.	2 wks. after 60 dys.
Holidays	7 paid	11 paid
Tuition Reimbursement	80%	100%
401k Retirement	Yes	Yes
Vacation Time	1-4 yrs. = 2 weeks 5-14 yrs. = 3 weeks	1-4 yrs. = 3 weeks 5-14 yrs. = 4 weeks
Laptop Computer	No	Yes
Travel	Within 25 miles	Yes
Cell Phone	Yes	Yes
Pager	Yes	Yes
On Call	Yes, 24 hours	No
Telecommuting (work @ home)	No	Yes
Car	Per Diem (uses own car)	Provided (plus maintenance and fuel)

Scott made an informed decision about a change in his career because he took the time to operationally define the meaning of the vague (non-operational) statement, *do I stay in the new bank or do I quit?* When Scott assumes his new position, he will be prepared to use the process to further define the aspects of the job that remain vague.

"What am I going to do?"

Susan:
Suddenly A Widow

Susan is 48 years old and lives with her 55-year-old husband, David, on a quiet residential street in Southern California. They have a 20-year-old son who attends college in the Midwest and a 16-year-old daughter enrolled in the local high school.

She is fortunate to have had the opportunity to stay at home during the children's early years. Six years ago David, an electrical engineer with a major construction company, was approached by their long-time friend Aaron to go into partnership with him. Three years earlier, Aaron, also an electrical engineer, started a contracting firm specializing in residential design. Aaron wanted to expand his business to include commercial building and needed a partner like David who had commercial experience.

The decision to join Aaron involved financial risks. It meant refinancing their home for $200,000, using $80,000 of their savings and Susan's returning to work. She did not mind having to go to work. However, she was nervous about the investment of all that money in the partnership.

She and David talked it over with the children. There was some initial grumbling about additional chores, housework and other financial adjustments that could alter their lifestyle. After their discussion everyone agreed it would have to be a team effort and each would accept the additional responsibilities.

Susan had a background in advertising. With the aid of a friend, she got a job as an Administrative Assistant in an independent advertising firm. During her six years with the company, she worked her way up to an account executive position, earning a gross salary of $60,000 a year including benefits. A year ago the agency downsized its staff. Susan's workload increased, and she was faced with a decision either to work longer hours or quit. She opted to stay. Recently a larger firm bought the agency and her job was eliminated. She accepted the new firm's offer of a severance package of four weeks' vacation and six weeks' salary amounting to $11,500.00.

Susan had an excellent reputation in her field and was quickly approached by several other agencies to work for them. David encouraged her to take some time off before she made a decision. A short break would not handicap them financially, nor adversely effect their ultimate goals for retirement. Their plans were for Susan to retire in another seven years, while David could semi-retire. The children would be out of college, working and/or married. She and David could travel and do the things they had placed on hold. Susan was looking forward to the future and as their 25th wedding anniversary approached life was hopeful and productive.

As she putters in her garden on this warm sunny day, she realizes how much she is enjoying a temporary break in her career. She hears the garden gate open and sees Aaron. By the look on his face she knows something is wrong. Aaron tells her he returned to the office to meet David for lunch. He found him lying on the office floor. When he didn't detect a pulse, he immediately called 911 and then David's doctor. David died on the way to the hospital.

Susan is in a state of disbelief and shock, hearing Aaron's words but unable to focus on the reality of their meaning. Her mind races: "He can't be dead. He can't just die!" She has to see him.

After they arrive at the hospital, she speaks to the doctor. He tells her that David had suffered a fatal heart attack. The doctor arranges for Aaron and Susan to see David. The sight of this once vibrant man, who has been her husband, lover, and best friend now lying lifeless, shatters her fragile control. She breaks down and can't stop crying.

Aaron suggests he take her home so she can be there when her daughter arrives from school. He calls her son at college and makes arrangements to fly him home. He also contacts her closest friend to help with the funeral arrangements. At this stage, Susan's mind is overcome with pain and grief. She tries to override her emotions. She knows she has to pull herself together for the children's sake.

Following the funeral Susan functions physically, but mentally she is still floating. She does manage to talk with her friends and David's business associates who are also in shock. It all seems so unreal.

Aaron calls on the Monday following the services, saying his and David's accountant wants to meet with them on Wednesday. Before she makes any personal decisions, the accountant needs to discuss various financial matters relative to the business. She knows official documents must be filed and the company's financial details need to be discussed. Susan realizes the meeting is inevitable, but why do they have to call it so soon after David's death?

Aaron drives her to the meeting. He gives her an overall picture of the business, with which she is unfamiliar. Susan listens but she doesn't hear. She is still in shock.

When the accountant presents the report of the company's financial status, she begins to feel her emotions rising to the surface. She finds it difficult to concentrate on the facts.

A. Four years ago the partnership had established a $300,000 line of credit. According to Aaron, he and David used all of their credit line to update their computer equipment. They hoped this would make them more competitive and increase their present and future sales. Unfortunately, in the past year, first the housing, then the commercial market took a sudden and steep decline. In the next 30 days the credit line will be up for renewal. Due to the decrease in the company's income, the bank may not renew the credit line. Either way Susan is responsible for $150,000 of the debt.

Susan is jolted into thinking about the facts being presented to her. She knew David and Aaron carried a survivor's insurance policy for $500,000 and questioned why that survival insurance will not cover this type of situation.

B. The accountant tells her that against his advice, the policy was canceled a year ago. David and Aaron told him the monthly payments were too costly.

Susan doesn't understand why David did not discuss the decision to cancel the policy with her.

C. Aaron informs her that David had canceled a $300,000 personal term life insurance policy. He says David couldn't keep up with the monthly payments.

Now she knows why she hasn't been able to find the policy among his personal papers. She just can't believe that David left her and the children without any financial protection. Why had he told Aaron and not her? Aaron cannot give her the answers she needs.

D. The accountant tells her that David also has a credit card debt in the amount of $28,000.

Aaron tells her David had not wanted to worry her about his financial problems. He had been using his credit card to give her $1,500 or more a month towards their household expenses, explaining that it was just part of his "draw" from the company.

As she listens, her emotions take over. She becomes angry, frustrated, and bewildered. She can no longer hold back her tears. Why hadn't David told her? It wasn't like him to keep problems from her. She could have helped. They could have worked something out together. Why had he encouraged her to take time off before starting a new job? She has many other questions, and he isn't here to answer them.

Susan thought she had control of her life. Now she doesn't know what she is going to do. There are so many debts she doesn't have the money to pay them. How could he do this to me?

The accountant gives her a breakdown of the business finances: the **(who, what, when, where, how, why and costs)** along with tax implications and other related information. He suggests she review the information. Since she handles the household budget, he asks her to provide him with a complete analysis of the family expenses. Once he reviews the additional information, along with the data on the tax returns, they and her lawyer will discuss what decisions need to be made regarding her financial situation.

Susan tells the accountant she can get back to him in two days with the data he requires. She decides not to discuss the financial situation with the children until she has all of the facts.

On the following day she makes an effort to take a calmer look at her situation. Susan has the written information from the accountant and a vague recollection of the conversations during the meeting. She needs to find an organized written method that will help her clarify her present situation. She remembered a *Ten-Step Guide To*

Analyze And Solve Problems (Refer to page 5) that she had used at work. Susan begins with **Step 1, recognize that a problem may exist.** The accountant and Aaron had informed her orally and in writing about the current financial situation of the business. She was also told that her husband had canceled his personal insurance policy.

She continues to **Step 2, analyze the background material and write a statement of the problem.** She reviews and investigates all the background material the accountant gave her related to the business problems: facts and opinions. She writes a general non-operational statement of the problem.

- *David left me with business and personal debts. I don't know what I am going to do.*

Susan proceeds to **Step 3, gather data to identify and prove a problem exists.** Susan needs to determine if there is a significant measurable difference between the event that should have happened (if David and Aaron had followed their original decisions) and what actually happened (decisions that altered the plan). (See Figure 6-1) She also needs to measure David's personal financial decisions. (See Figure 6-2, page 92)

Figure 6-1
David and Aaron's Financial
Business Decisions

---

1. $300,000 LINE OF CREDIT WITH
   THE BANK

   Event that Should have Happened:
   Not to use OVER 25% of their entire credit line.

   Event that Happened:
   Aaron and David used $300,000 credit line.

   Deviation Between Events:
   75%

2. PARTNERSHIP SURVIVAL INSURANCE
   POLICY

   Event that Should have Happened:
   Maintain $500,000 Policy.

   Event that Happened:
   Cancellation of $500,000 Policy.

   Deviation Between Events:
   100%

Figure 6-2
David's Personal Financial Decisions

---

1. DAVID'S CREDIT CARD DEBT

    Event that Should have Happened:
    Zero use of credit card to maintain household expenses.

    Event that Happened:
    $28,000 debt incurred.

    Deviation is 100%

2. PERSONAL LIFE INSURANCE POLICY

    Event that Should have Happened:
    Maintain $300,000 Life Insurance Policy.

    Event that Happened:
    Cancellation of $300,000 Life Insurance Policy.

    Deviation is 100%

An analysis reveals the deviations are significant and prove a problem exists. However, the data does not reveal the cause of the problem: "why" the plans were changed?

Susan continues to **Step 4, gather additional data.** She needs to focus on getting an exact accounting of her personal finances. She accesses the household records in her computer. In a matter of seconds she retrieves the information.

Currently it costs $1,850 a month for utilities and mortgage payments to run the house, plus $200 a month towards her son's rent at college. He is on a full sports scholarship and has a part-time job to cover his daily expenses. Her daughter will receive Social Security benefits in the amount of $400 a month that will help with the bulk of her expenses. Susan needs approximately $1,000 a month for food, dry cleaning, gasoline and personal spending money. A summary of the expenses shows she needs $3,050 a month to pay for her and the children's current living expenses.

Susan has $15,000 in a money-market account and $1,250 in her checking account. There is also a $10,000 life insurance policy, which David had not canceled, and a medical insurance policy that covers the cost of the funeral and hospital expenses. Susan has a 401K in the amount of $20,000. She faxes the data to the accountant so he can integrate the household data with the business data.

She telephones their insurance agent to find out how David could have canceled the personal policy without her knowledge. The agent informs her that not only was the policy in David's name, but he was the owner of the policy with Susan as beneficiary. As the owner of the policy he could cancel without her signature. Susan didn't remember the agent or David explaining that information to her when the policy was written.

The tears begin to flow again. She has no job. No income and she is responsible for her children and herself. However, she knows from experience that if she concentrates objectively on the tasks at hand and focuses her energy into action, she will not fall into the emotional trap of being mentally paralyzed.

But right now she needs to rest, to be alone, and to gather her strength. Susan will have to explain the situation to the children, although she will not be able to explain the "why" of David's decisions.

During her discussion with the children her son offers to take a year off from college and go to work. Susan is determined he remain in school. Both children promise to cut down on their expenses.

She decides to attend only to those problems which involve her survival and over which she has some immediate control. How is she going to pay back David's business debts? She has to return to work as soon as possible or all of her savings will be gone. A week later Susan calls the agencies that had contacted her after her job had been eliminated. All but one of the agencies have filled their positions.

The interview with the remaining agency goes well. She knows most of the people at the agency and while the procedures and clients are somewhat different, the work is familiar. It will be a change but not a drastic one. The agency offered her $62,000 a year with benefits. She is asked to report to work in two weeks.

Susan decides to postpone making any decisions about the house. With the income from her new position she can continue to make the mortgage payments. Susan feels she wants to keep the house and will sell only if her job doesn't work out. She is not ready for any more changes in her life.

A week before Susan starts her new job, Aaron calls and tells her it is urgent that he meet with her. The accountant and her lawyer will be there. He has a written proposal to present to her, and he will give her the details at the meeting. She agrees.

Aaron has been working with the banker to extend the repayment time on the credit line. He gave the banker signed contracts he had obtained for two new residential housing projects. They are scheduled to begin next month with a completion date of four months. The projects are estimated to net $175,000. The banker will give Aaron an additional six months if he receives, within forty-eight hours, a signed agreement between Susan and Aaron that states the final settlement of the partnership.

Aaron presents Susan with the following two options:

Option 1. Retain David's one-half interest in the partnership. She can keep her job and work with Aaron part-time to develop a new marketing and sales program. She can also assist with the administrative work. After the loan is reduced she will receive a draw from the business. The amount to be determined later.

There is the potential for additional contracts. Aaron is in negotiation with five residential building companies who are all close to issuing contracts for an estimated total of $1,000,000 within the year.

Option 2. Relinquish her one-half of the partnership and Aaron will assume her liability for $150,000 credit line and any other outstanding business expenses. He will also pay her $25,000 next year and $75,000 over a period of three years (discounted amount) for inventory and equipment. A payment schedule is to be determined by the future income. Susan will not receive any other financial compensation and will be released from all financial and legal obligations of the partnership.

Susan has to make a decision within forty-eight hours. She resumes her analysis with **Step 5, review and summarize the collected data.** Susan organizes, examines and summarizes all of the financial data she has from Aaron, her accountant and the bank to be certain all the vital information she has is complete and accurate. She then proceeds to **Step 6, evaluate the data.** As she evaluates the data she is caught between her desire to salvage what she and David had begun and to find a way to rid herself of the financial burden.

She continues to **Step 7, write a statement of the possible action that could be taken to solve the problem** before she chooses one of Aaron's two options.

- *Should I retain one-half interest in the partnership or relinquish my one-half of the partnership to Aaron?*

Susan proceeds to **Step 8, state the criteria that a solution to the problem must meet.** Susan establishes her criteria: not to increase my present business debt of $150,000.

She continues to **Step 9, develop options to solve the problem.** Because of the bank's forty-eight hour time limit she doesn't have time to consider further options.

Option one requires Susan to retain her one-half interest in the partnership. On the positive side if the business recovers and expands in a year or two, she might be able to double her investment and then sell her half for a profit and recover all or part of their original investment of $280,000.

The disadvantage of option one is if Aaron doesn't get the potential new contracts she may be forced to sell her home to obtain the funds to pay off her half-interest in the business. She isn't certain she is emotionally strong enough to cope with participation in the business, hold down a new, full-time job and still spend needed time with her daughter. Another consideration is her dissatisfaction with Aaron's explanations as to the logic of his and David's financial decisions.

Option two requires her to relinquish her half of the partnership to Aaron. She will rid herself of the credit line debt of $150,000 and any other outstanding business expenses and debts. There is also the possibility that business will increase to the point that Aaron will pay her $25,000 next year and $75,000 over a period of three years. She will not recover all of their original investment of $280,000 in the partnership.

The disadvantage of option two is if the business fails she might lose $100,000.

She proceeds to **Step 10, select a preferred option to solve the problem.** She selects option two, to accept Aaron's offer to relinquish one-half of the partnership to him. The decision meets her criteria.

The process of *operational analysis* helped Susan keep her emotional pain from overwhelming her ability to make an objective decision. She was able to focus her attention long enough to gather the data she needed to make a quick decision without knowing the cause of the problem.

Practice, Practice, Practice

When you think of the word **"practice,"** do you visualize repeating a task to develop a skill so that it becomes a routine part of your thought process? You can apply the same procedure to enhance your ability to recognize the difference between *operational* and *non-operational language* – a key to problem solving. Here are three ways:

1. **Review the six stories.**

   - Are there additional questions you would ask about each non-operational problem statement?
     Do these questions reinforce your beliefs or are they objective questions?
     Are you able to operationally define the answers to your questions?

2. **Examine your personal and/or business correspondence.**

- Do you find in your personal and household-related correspondence you use more non-operational language than in your business-related correspondence?

- When, where and why do you use non-operational terms? Do you use adjectives and adverbs to provide the reader with a visual picture of events? Or, do you use concrete nouns and active verbs to relate the facts of events?

- Is there a pattern to your use of operational and/or non-operational terms?

3. **Observe/listen to the media.**

- How are events, positive and negative, throughout the world being reported? Is factual (operational) or emotional (non-operational) language being used?

A Thought

To Find the Truth of a Problem
Gives You the Knowledge to Act

About the Authors

Jeanette A. Griver

Jeanette Griver is founder and Chief Executive Officer of Compsych Systems, Inc., a human factors corporation that specializes in applied research, consulting and training.

She is an international consultant and since 1964 has presented her communication and problem-solving techniques to more than 50,000 people on three continents.

Ms. Griver received her B.A. in Psychology from the College of Letters and Science at the University of California at Los Angeles and her M.A. in Human Factors Psychology from the College of Letters and Science at the University of Southern California.

Michele W. Vodrey

Michele Vodrey is a native Californian and continues to reside in Los Angeles. She attended college in New York where she majored in English and Theatre Arts.

She is a consultant, writer and editor and for the past twenty years has been associated with Compsych Systems, Inc.

Ms. Vodrey is co-editor of *Applied Problem Analysis Plus*, a problem solving book for people in business, government and the professions.